# JESUS, DIVINE AND HUMAN

He agonized in the Garden and cried out in what sounds like utter despair on the Cross. Why then has Christendom been persuaded not merely to admire Him, but, as it has done for centuries, to worship Him?

It cannot have been merely because He was supposed by His followers to have risen from the dead, for He appeared to none but His friends. It was not perhaps surprising that *they* should believe, but how did they persuade people who had watched Him die, without a scrap of evidence except their bare word to support them? The only explanation that can be given, surely, is that men and women who had been in contact with Him before had felt Him to be the kind of person about whom to believe that He had risen from the dead was not impossible. A very different character, the Roman emperor Nero, exercised an uncanny power over the imagination of many of his contemporaries. But what was believed about Nero was that he had never died. In the case of Jesus of Nazareth, the very crowds who had seen Him die supported the apostles in their assertions about the Resurrection of the Crucified so strongly that the authorities who had been responsible for His crucifixion, though willing to wound, were afraid to strike, and to all intents and purposes were powerless against them. Even if we may allow for a little exaggeration of their triumph by those who figured so bravely in it, the fact remains that the Church did get itself started, and in Jerusalem, the scene of its complete collapse, within a few weeks of the Crucifixion.

Strangely enough, the very theologians who are

readiest to emphasize the importance of the message He brought, and insist that with His coming God entered into the world so decisively that every man and nation who has ever heard of it is judged by his response or lack of response to its challenge, also tell us that we can know little or nothing of Jesus of Nazareth, that what we have in the Gospels is not an accurate account of His sayings or doings, much less His complete life-story, but an account of what the Church of the first or second generation had come to believe about Him. We are told that, before any of our evangelists put pen to paper, stories about Jesus had been handled by preachers for a generation, every one of them interested not at all in historical accuracy, but in getting their hearers converted to the belief that 'there is no other name given under Heaven by which we must be saved' (Acts iv. 12). When we remember how inevitably stories grow as they pass from lip to lip, even when the narrators are anxious to repeat exactly what was told them, we realize how much more radically they are likely to change when they have a propagandist motive behind them, and the original eye-witnesses who might be able to check the exuberance of pious imagination are dead or absent.

What the form-critics, as they have been called, tell us about the psychology of propagandists is true, and they have rendered invaluable service in reminding us of facts about human nature to which much study of the synoptic problem may blind us. At the lowest computation there *is* a gap of more than twenty years between the Resurrection and the earliest connected story of the events of Easter Day that has come miracles – far from it – but simply because they did not follow the apostolic tradition. People wanted to know more about the boyhood of Jesus, and to have a more exciting story of the events of Good Friday and Easter Day, and, of course, the supply was forthcoming to meet the demand. Moreover, the general level of intelligence in the early Church cannot have been high, and there was no central authority allowing some books to be read in Christian meetings and forbidding others.

Yet somehow before the end of the second century Irenaeus can say that there can only be four Gospels, as there are four points of the compass. Apostolic tradition must surely have been much more solid and coherent than these scholars are generally willing to admit. In many respects the four Gospels must have been, from the point of view of rank-and-file members of the Church, exceedingly disappointing; they have little to say about Jesus as a boy, they refuse to dwell on lurid or pathetic details of His Crucifixion, and none of them attempts an account of the actual rising of Jesus from the tomb. Above all, they represent Him as often angry and surprised; they picture Him stricken with a mortal sorrow in face of death, and – apparently – despairing altogether on the Cross. None of these features of the narrative could easily be fitted into a convincing popular picture of the strong Son of God. However much they may mean to us, we have plenty of evidence that they caused deep offence to less sophisticated readers. If, in spite of these handicaps, they could with such comparative ease and swiftness have driven their more exciting rivals from

the field, it can only have been because the leaders
of the Church had a very clear idea of what was and
what was not 'apostolic', and that the eye-witnesses to
whom Luke refers in the preface to his Gospel lived
long enough and travelled widely enough to leave a
definite impression behind, not only of the time when
the ministry of Jesus began, and the details of its cul-
mination on Calvary, but also some outline of the
general course of events between these two fixed
points.

Most form-critics would agree, I suppose, that the
outline of the Passion story in the four Gospels is so
uniform that an apostolic narrative must lie behind it.
It need never have existed in writing, but it was at
least firm and concrete enough to act as an effective
check upon pious imagination.    When we think of
the complete absence of any striving for effect in the
account of the Crucifixion itself, of the bare statement –
common to all four Gospels – that 'they crucified
Him', without the slightest effort to heighten the
agony, or even to describe the nailing of hands and
feet, and then turn to the 'Gospel of Peter' (early
second century), with its statement that when 'they
crucified Him, the Lord kept silence, as feeling no
pain', its account of what happened during the hours
of darkness, its change of 'My God, My God, why
hast Thou forsaken Me?' to 'My power, My power,
why hast thou forsaken Me?' we are in a different
world.   Surely, if preachers had really felt free to
decorate the stories which had come down to them, to
remove difficulties, and give their hearers the kind of
Jesus they wanted, the Passion and Resurrection stories

as we know them would have been unrecognizable before the end of the first generation, the very time when
our Gospels began to be written.

We are forced back, it seems to me, to the bare
alternative; either Peter (with help from one or more
Johns) made the Jesus who has captured and held the
attention of Christendom for nineteen centuries, or
Jesus made Peter. For we must not forget that, when
we speak of 'apostolic tradition', we are not thinking
of any kind of authoritative Scripture, but of a small
group of men who professed to have been disciples of
Jesus and witnesses of His Resurrection. None of our
Gospels comes directly from any one of this small
group. Who were these men who, perhaps, without
putting pen to paper, were able so to stamp their
personal testimony on the four books we call the
Gospels, that they have concentrated the adoration
of the centuries upon their Hero? No other classics
have been so ruthlessly dissected; every word of
Mark's Gospel has time after time been subjected
to microscopical analysis; his sentences have been
pulled to pieces and rearranged in a thousand ways.
Yet the book lives; its very fragments have feet and
hands to carry a man away with.

Any simple Christian who takes the trouble to read
through Schweitzer's *Quest of the Historical Jesus* can
hardly be blamed for feeling that little or nothing is
left; yet out of the ruins the author is able in his last
two chapters to build up a portrait of Jesus of Nazareth
which not only stirs the soul, but can change a man's
own life in a moment, and actually did carry Schweitzer himself from a unique position of influence in the

universities of Europe as theologian, philosopher, musician and literary critic, to a lonely hospital in the African jungle.  One of the most advanced of the form-critics, Bultmann, deals more drastically still with the Gospel-records of the life of Jesus, yet in his *Jesus and the Word* he too is able, from the few fragments he leaves us, to make us feel that, in meeting Jesus, we are face to face with destiny.  The very men who deny most insistently that we can know anything for certain about the details of the life of Jesus prove His power over their own souls.  Indeed, the most moving books about the Gospels in the last twenty years or so have not been written by simple believers, but by men who first exasperate us by their scepticism, and then subdue us by their devotion.  It would seem that the Gospels have this at least in common with those low forms of life which infest our gardens; however much you cut them up, they live on; they are fearfully and wonderfully alive.  I have seen too many men's minds come to flower in a week at the touch of the Jesus of history, as He is revealed in the Gospels, to doubt that the explanation of the miracle in all three cases – with the evangelists, the modern critic, and the theological student fresh from the farm or the counter – is the same; there is life-changing power in any kind of contact with this 'greatest of the sons of men' who is 'God manifest in the flesh'; 'there is life', in a sense not imagined by the hymn-writer, 'for a look at the Crucified One', life for the mind and body as well as for the soul, for dormant imagination as truly as for paralysed will.

To suggest that this endlessly self-propagating